Wisdom

from

THE
HIDDEN LIFE
OF TREES

PETER WOHLLEBEN

Translated by
JANE BILLINGHURST

Wisdom

from

THE HIDDEN LIFE
OF TREES

DAVID SUZUKI INSTITUTE

GREYSTONE BOOKS
Vancouver/Berkeley/London

Contents

— 1 —
**William Trost
Richards**
Indian Summer | 1875

— 2/3 —
**Johann Heinrich
Schilbach**
*Wooded Shore at the
King Lake (Königsee)*
FIRST HALF 19TH CENTURY

— 4 —
Julian Alden Weir
The Red Bridge
(detail) | 1895

Introduction

I have been a forester for over twenty years, and my observations will help you learn about the lives of trees and discover what we share in common. I encourage you to look around where you live. What dramas are being played out in wooded areas you can explore?

This book is a lens to help you take a closer look at what you might have taken for granted. Slow down, breathe deep, and look around. What can you hear? What do you see? How do you feel?

Trees are important, but when trees unite to create a fully functioning forest, you really can say that the whole is greater than its parts. Forests matter at a more fundamental level than most of us realize.

After you flip through these pages, a walk in the woods will never be the same again.

PETER WOHLLEBEN

⟨ **Christoph Nathe** | *A Waterfall in a Forest at Langhennersdorf* | LATE 18TH–EARLY 19TH CENTURY

Henry Farrer | *Winter Scene in Moonlight* | 1869

A Tree Is Not a Forest

On its own, a tree cannot establish a consistent local climate. It is at the mercy of wind and weather. But together, many trees create an ecosystem that moderates extremes of heat and cold, stores a great deal of water, and generates a great deal of humidity. The community must remain intact no matter what. If every tree were looking out only for itself, then quite a few of them would never reach old age. Regular fatalities would result in many large gaps in the tree canopy, which would make it easier for storms to get inside the forest and uproot more trees.

Every tree, therefore, is valuable to the community and worth keeping around for as long as possible. And that is why even sick individuals are supported and nourished until they recover.

Joseph Bartholomew Kidd
Rose-Breasted Grosbeak | MID-LATE 19TH CENTURY

Registering Pain

Beeches, spruce, and oaks all register pain as soon as some creature starts nibbling on them. When a caterpillar takes a hearty bite out of a leaf, the tissue around the site of the damage changes. In addition, the leaf tissue sends out electrical signals, just as human tissue does when it is hurt. It takes an hour or so before defensive compounds reach the leaves to spoil the pest's meal. Trees live their lives in the really slow lane, even when they are in danger. But this slow tempo doesn't mean that a tree is not on top of what is happening in different parts of its structure. If the roots find themselves in trouble, this information is broadcast throughout the tree, which can trigger the leaves to release scent compounds. And not just any old scent compounds, but compounds that are specifically formulated for the task at hand.

Your trees may not function

exactly as my trees do,

and your forest might look

a little different, but the

underlying narrative is the same.

Paul Klee | *Park* | 1920

Unidentified | *Landscape* | N.D.

A Multipronged Defense

Oaks carry bitter, toxic tannins in their bark and leaves. These either kill chewing insects outright or at least affect the leaves' taste to such an extent that instead of being deliciously crunchy, they become biliously bitter.

Trees don't rely exclusively on dispersal in the air, for if they did, some neighbors would not get wind of the danger. Dr. Suzanne Simard of the University of British Columbia has discovered that they also warn each other using chemical signals sent through the fungal networks around their root tips, which operate no matter what the weather. Surprisingly, news bulletins are sent via the roots not only by means of chemical compounds but also by means of electrical impulses. Once the latest news has been broadcast, all oaks in the area promptly pump tannins through their veins.

Henri Rousseau | *Virgin Forest with Sunset—*
Negro Attacked by a Jaguar | 1910

A Sense of Taste

When it comes to some species of insects, trees can accurately identify which bad guys they are up against. The saliva of each species is different, and trees can match the saliva to the insect. Indeed, the match can be so precise that trees can release pheromones that summon specific beneficial predators. The beneficial predators help trees by eagerly devouring the insects that are bothering them. For example, elms and pines call on small parasitic wasps that lay their eggs inside leaf-eating caterpillars. As the wasp larvae develop, they devour the caterpillars bit by bit from the inside out. Not a nice way to die. The result, however, is that the trees are saved from bothersome pests and can keep growing with no further damage. The fact that trees can recognize saliva is, incidentally, evidence for yet another skill they must have. For if they can identify saliva, they must also have a sense of taste.

Mogens Ballin | *Wood with Crooked Tree* | 1891-92

Interdependence

Most individual trees of the same species growing in the same stand are connected to each other through their root systems. It appears that nutrient exchange and helping neighbors in times of need is the rule.

Paul Sébillot | *Spring in Brittany* | 1874

Mossy Stones

Years ago, I stumbled across some strange-looking mossy stones in one of the preserves of old beech trees that grow in the forest I manage. Casting my mind back, I realized I had passed by them many times before without paying them any heed. But that day, I stopped and bent down to take a good look. The stones were an unusual shape: they were gently curved with hollowed-out areas. Carefully, I lifted the moss on one of the stones. What I found underneath was tree bark. So, these were not stones, but old wood.

I took out my pocketknife and scraped away some of the bark until I got down to a greenish layer. Green? That could mean only one thing: this piece of wood was still alive! What I had stumbled upon were the gnarled remains of an enormous ancient tree stump. Living cells must have food in the form of sugar, they must breathe, and they must grow, at least a little. But without leaves—and therefore without photosynthesis—that's impossible. It must be getting assistance from neighboring trees. I didn't want to injure the old stump by digging around it, but one thing was clear: the surrounding beeches were pumping sugar to the stump to keep it alive.

Tree Partners

Do tree societies have second-class citizens? It seems they do, though the idea of "class" doesn't quite fit. It is rather the degree of connection—or maybe even affection—that decides how helpful a tree's colleagues will be.

You can check this out for yourself simply by looking up into the forest canopy. The average tree grows its branches out until it encounters the branch tips of a neighboring tree of the same height. It doesn't grow any wider because the air and better light in this space are already taken. However, it heavily reinforces the branches it has extended. You get the impression that there's quite a shoving match going on up there. But a pair of true friends is careful right from the outset not to grow overly thick branches in each other's direction. The trees don't want to take anything away from each other, and so they develop sturdy branches only at the outer edges of their crowns, that is to say, only in the direction of "non-friends." Such partners are often so tightly connected at the roots that sometimes they even die together.

⟨ **Adrian Ludwig Richter** | *Genoveva* | 1872

Carl August Lebschee | *Wooded Landscape with Stag* | 1800-77

Scent Messages

Four decades ago, scientists noticed that giraffes on the African savannah were feeding on umbrella thorn acacias. It took the acacias mere minutes to start pumping toxic substances into their leaves to rid themselves of the large herbivores. The giraffes got the message and moved on to other trees in the vicinity. But did they move on to trees close by? No, they walked right by a few trees and resumed their meal only when they had moved about 100 yards away.

The acacia trees that were being eaten gave off a warning gas that signaled to neighboring trees of the same species that a crisis was at hand. Right away, all the forewarned trees also pumped toxins into their leaves to prepare themselves. The giraffes therefore moved farther away to a part of the savannah where they could find trees that were oblivious to what was going on.

Abel Rodríguez | *Seasonal Changes
in the Flooded Rainforest* | 2009-10

Gustav Klimt | *Rosebushes under the Trees* | 1905

Spreading the News

Fungi in the forest floor operate like fiber-optic Internet cables. Their thin filaments penetrate the ground, weaving through it in almost unbelievable density. One teaspoon of forest soil contains many miles of these "hyphae." Over centuries, a single fungus can cover many square miles and network an entire forest. The fungal connections transmit signals from one tree to the next, helping the trees exchange news about insects, drought, and other dangers. Science has adopted a term first coined by the journal *Nature* for Dr. Suzanne Simard's discovery of the "wood wide web."

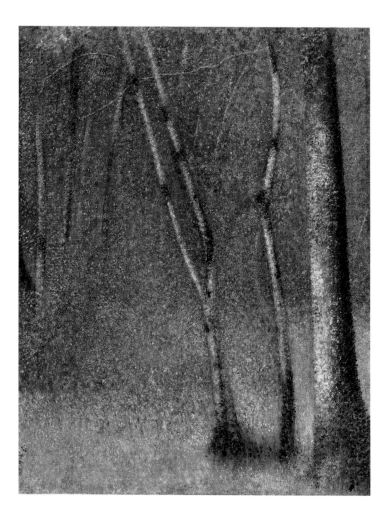

Georges Seurat | *The Forest at Pontaubert* | 1881

Radio Silence

If trees are weakened, it could be that they lose their conversational skills along with their ability to defend themselves. Otherwise, it's difficult to explain why insect pests specifically seek out trees whose health is already compromised. It's conceivable that to do this, insects listen to trees' urgent chemical warnings and then test trees that don't pass the message on by taking a bite out of their leaves or bark. A tree's silence could be because of a serious illness or, perhaps, the loss of its fungal network, which would leave the tree completely cut off from the latest news. The tree no longer registers approaching disaster, and the doors are open for the caterpillar and beetle buffet.

Thanks to selective breeding, our cultivated plants have, for the most part, lost their ability to communicate above or below ground. Isolated by their silence, they are easy prey for insect pests. That is one reason why modern agriculture uses so many pesticides. Perhaps farmers can learn from the forests and breed a little more wildness back into their grain and potatoes so that they'll be more talkative in the future.

Soundscapes

Along with colleagues from Bristol and Florence, Dr. Monica Gagliano from the University of Western Australia has, quite literally, had her ear to the ground. It's not practical to study trees in the laboratory; therefore, researchers substitute grain seedlings. It didn't take them long to discover that the roots were crackling quietly at a frequency of 220 hertz. Crackling roots? That doesn't necessarily mean anything. After all, even dead wood crackles when it's burned in a stove. But the noises caused the researchers to sit up and pay attention. For the roots of seedlings not directly involved in the experiment reacted. Whenever the seedlings' roots were exposed to a crackling at 220 hertz, they oriented their tips in that direction. That means the grasses were registering this frequency, so it makes sense to say they "heard" it.

⟨ Unidentified (British) copy after
Sir Joshua Reynolds | *Mrs. Lloyd* | 18TH CENTURY

Julie de Graag | *Moon Light* | 1920

Connecting to
the Wood Wide Web

To enter into a partnership with one of the many thousands of kinds of fungi, a tree must be very open—literally—because the fungal threads grow into its soft root hairs. The fungus not only penetrates and envelops the tree's roots, but also allows its web to roam through the surrounding forest floor. In so doing, it extends the reach of the tree's own roots as the web grows out toward other trees. Here, it connects with other trees' fungal partners and roots. And so a network is created, and now it's easy for the trees to exchange vital nutrients and even information—such as an impending insect attack.

Lawrence Paul Yuxweluptun | *New Climate Landscape
(Northwest Coast Climate Change)* | 2019

The Next Generation

A mother tree reaches the end of her life. As the tree hits the ground, it snaps a couple of waiting seedlings. The gap in the canopy gives the remaining seedlings the green light, and they can begin photosynthesizing to their hearts' content. Now their metabolism gets into gear, and the trees grow sturdier leaves and needles that can withstand and metabolize bright light.

This stage lasts between one and three years. Once it is over, it's time to get a move on. All the youngsters want to grow now, and only those that go for it and grow straight as an arrow toward the sky are still in the race. The cards are stacked against those free spirits who think they can meander right or left as the mood takes them and dawdle before they stretch upward. Overtaken by their comrades, they find themselves in the shadows once again. The difference is that it is even darker under the leaves of their cohort that has pulled ahead than it was under their mothers. The teenagers use up the greater part of what weak light remains; the stragglers give up the ghost and become humus once again.

As the bright sunlight stimulates growth, their buds become sweet, tasty treats—at least as far as the deer are concerned. Flowering plants also try their luck. By coiling itself around the trunk, honeysuckle can keep up with the growth of a young tree and its flowers can bask in the sun. However, the coiling vine cuts into the expanding bark and slowly strangles the little tree. Will the canopy formed by the old trees close and plunge the little trees into darkness once again? If it does, the honeysuckle will wither away, leaving only scars.

The young trees that continue to grow will have their patience tested yet again before another twenty years have passed. For this is how long it takes for the dead mother's neighbors to grow their branches out into the gap she left when she fell. Once the upper story grows over, it is dark once again down below. All the trees that have made it as far as the middle story are now the crown princes and princesses who, at the next opportunity, will finally be allowed to grow up.

⟩ **Paul Gauguin** | *Te burao (The Hibiscus Tree)* | 1892

William Turner | *Study of a Tree in Bloom* | c. 1835

This Way for Sugar!

Blossoms do not release scent at random or to please us. Fruit trees, willows, and chestnuts use their olfactory missives to draw attention to themselves and invite passing bees to sate themselves. Sweet nectar, a sugar-rich liquid, is the reward the insects get in exchange for the incidental dusting they receive while they visit. The form and color of blossoms are signals, as well. They act somewhat like a billboard that stands out against the general green of the tree canopy and points the way to a snack.

Kamal-ol-Molk | *The Doshan Tappeh Street* | 1899

E.A. Séguy | *Tree Pochoir Pattern in Oriental Style* (detail) | c. 1914

46

Memory Making

Mimosas are tropical creeping herbs. When they are touched, they close their feathery little leaves to protect themselves. Australian scientist Dr. Monica Gagliano designed an experiment where individual drops of water fell on the plants' foliage at regular intervals. At first, the anxious leaves closed immediately, but after a while, the little plants learned there was no danger of damage from the water droplets. After that, the leaves remained open despite the drops. Even more surprising for Gagliano was the fact that the mimosas could remember and apply their lesson weeks later, even without any further tests.

The thickness and stability
of a trunk build up as
the tree responds to a series
of aches and pains.
In a natural forest, this little
game can be repeated many times
over the lifetime of a tree.

Unidentified | *The Tree of Life* | FIRST HALF 17TH CENTURY

49

Asher B. Durand | *Woodland Glen* | c. 1850-55

Upbringing

Young beech trees are so keen on growing quickly that it would be no problem at all for them to grow about 18 inches taller per season. Unfortunately for them, their own mothers do not approve of rapid growth. They shade their offspring with their enormous crowns, and the crowns of all the mature trees form a thick canopy over the forest floor. This canopy lets only 3 percent of available sunlight reach the ground and, therefore, their children's leaves. With that amount of sunlight, a tree can photosynthesize just enough to keep its own body from dying. There's nothing left to fuel a decent drive upward or even a thicker trunk.

Thanks to slow growth, their inner woody cells are tiny and contain almost no air. That makes the trees flexible and resistant to breaking in storms. Even more important is their heightened resistance to fungi, which have difficulty spreading through the tough little trunks.

Friedrich Christian Klass | *Landscape
with Waterfall* | LATE 18TH-EARLY 19TH CENTURY

Tree Etiquette

In the forest, there are unwritten guidelines for tree etiquette. These guidelines lay down the proper appearance and acceptable forms of behavior. A mature, well-behaved deciduous tree has a ramrod-straight trunk with a regular, orderly arrangement of wood fibers. The roots stretch out evenly in all directions and reach down into the earth under the tree. In its youth, the tree had narrow branches extending sideways from its trunk. They died back a long time ago, and the tree sealed them off with fresh bark and new wood so that what you see now is a long, smooth column. Only when you get to the top do you see a symmetrical crown formed of strong branches angling upward like arms raised to heaven. An ideally formed tree such as this can grow to be very old.

Johann Wilhelm Schirmer | *Mountainous
Landscape with a River* | 1835-37

Silent Screams

When trees are really thirsty, they begin to scream. If you're out in the forest, you won't be able to hear them, because this all takes place at ultrasonic levels. Scientists at the Swiss Federal Institute for Forest, Snow, and Landscape Research recorded the sounds, and this is how they explain them: Vibrations occur in the trunk when the flow of water from the roots to the leaves is interrupted. This is a purely mechanical event and it probably doesn't mean anything. And yet?

We know how the sounds are produced, and if we were to look through a microscope to examine how humans produce sounds, what we would see wouldn't be that different: the passage of air down the windpipe causes our vocal cords to vibrate. When I think about the research results, it seems to me that these vibrations could indeed be much more than just vibrations—they could be cries of thirst. The trees might be screaming out a dire warning to their colleagues that water levels are running low.

Trees maintain
an inner balance.
They budget their strength
carefully, and they must
be economical with energy
so that they can meet
all their needs. They expend
some energy growing.

Advancing Age

Every tree gradually stops growing taller. Its roots and vascular system cannot pump water and nutrients any higher because this exertion would be too much for the tree. Instead, the tree just gets wider (like many people of advancing years...). At first, it can no longer manage to feed its topmost twigs, and these die off. And so, just as an old person gradually loses body mass, an old tree does too. The next storm sweeps the dead twigs out of the crown, and after this cleanup, the tree looks a little fresher for a while. The process is repeated each year, reducing the crown so gradually we barely notice. Once all the topmost twigs and small branches are lost, only the thicker lower branches remain. Eventually, they die too. Now the tree can no longer hide its advanced age or its infirmity.

⟨ **J. Alden Weir** | *(Landscape)* | AFTER 1900

Johann Christoph Rist | *Landscape with a Waterfall* | 1816

A Giant Water Pump

Scientists studied different forests around the world and everywhere the results were the same. It didn't matter if they were studying a rain forest or the Siberian taiga, it was always the trees that were transferring life-giving moisture into land-locked interiors.

⟩ Johann Georg Wagner | *The Morning* | 1732-67

What Is a Tree Exactly?

Trees are majestic beings, under whose crowns we seem as insignificant as ants in the grass, right? But on a journey to Lapland, I stumbled upon completely different ambassadors of the tree family that made me feel like Gulliver in Lilliput. I'm talking about dwarf trees on the tundra, which are sometimes trampled to death by travelers who don't even know they are there. It can take these trees a hundred years to grow just 8 inches tall. Science doesn't recognize them as trees.

And what if you cut a tree down? Is it then dead? What about a centuries-old stump that is still alive today, thanks to its comrades? Is that a tree? And, if it isn't, then what is it?

⟨ **Paul Cézanne** | *The Bend in the Road* | 1900-6

Caspar David Friedrich | *Statue of the*
Madonna in the Mountains | 1804

The Root of the Matter

The oldest spruce in Dalarna province in Sweden has grown a carpet of flat shrubby growth around its single small trunk.

Research revealed the spruce to be an absolutely unbelievable 9,550 years old. The individual shoots were younger, but these new growths from the past few centuries were not considered to be stand-alone trees but part of a larger whole. And, I think, quite rightly so. After all, it is the root that has withstood severe changes in climatic conditions. And it is the root that has regrown trunks time and time again. It is in the roots that centuries of experience are stored, and it is this experience that has allowed the tree's survival to the present day.

William Henry Fox Talbot | *Kasuga*
Deer Mandala | LATE 14TH CENTURY

70

Can Plants Think?

In conjunction with his colleagues, František Baluška from the Institute of Cellular and Molecular Botany at the University of Bonn believes brain-like structures can be found at root tips. In addition to signaling pathways, there are also numerous systems and molecules similar to those found in animals. When a root feels its way forward in the ground, it is aware of stimuli. The researchers measured electrical signals that led to changes in behavior after the signals were processed in a "transition zone." If the root encounters toxic substances, impenetrable stones, or saturated soil, it analyzes the situation and transmits the necessary adjustments to the growing tip. The root tip changes direction as a result of this communication and steers the growing root around the critical areas.

Right now, most plant researchers are skeptical about whether such behavior points to a repository for intelligence, the faculty of memory, and emotions. Among other things, they get worked up about carrying over findings in similar situations with animals and, at the end of the day, about how this threatens to blur the boundary between plants and animals. And so what? What would be so awful about that?

Vincent van Gogh | *Cypresses* | 1889

The Vitality of Age

The older the tree, the more quickly it grows. Trees with trunks 3 feet in diameter generate three times as much biomass as trees that are only half as wide. So, in the case of trees, being old doesn't mean being weak, bowed, and fragile. Quite the opposite, it means being full of energy and highly productive. In older trees, fungi can lead to rot inside the trunk, but this doesn't slow future growth one little bit. If we want to use forests as a weapon in the fight against climate change, then we must allow them to grow old, which is exactly what large conservation groups are asking us to do.

Beetle mites, springtails,

and pseudocentipedes are not

nearly as engaging as orangutans

or humpback whales, but

in the forest, these little guys

are the first link in the food chain

and can, therefore, be

considered terrestrial plankton.

F. Hopkinson Smith

75

Unidentified | *Amitabha, the Buddha of
the Western Pure Land (Sukhavati)* | c. 1700

Storing Carbon

The forest is a gigantic carbon dioxide vacuum that constantly filters out and stores this component of the air. Some of this carbon dioxide returns to the atmosphere after a tree's death, but most of it remains locked in the ecosystem forever. A crumbling trunk is gradually gnawed and munched into smaller and smaller pieces and worked, by fractions of inches, more deeply into the soil. The rain takes care of whatever is left, as it flushes organic remnants down into the soil. The farther underground, the cooler it is. And as the temperature falls, life slows down, until it comes almost to a standstill. And so it is that carbon dioxide finds its final resting place in the form of humus, which continues to become more concentrated as it ages. In the far distant future, it might even become coal.

Wouldn't it be beautiful and meaningful if we allowed our trees to follow in the footsteps of their ancestors by giving them the opportunity to recapture at least some of the carbon dioxide released by power plants and store it in the ground once again?

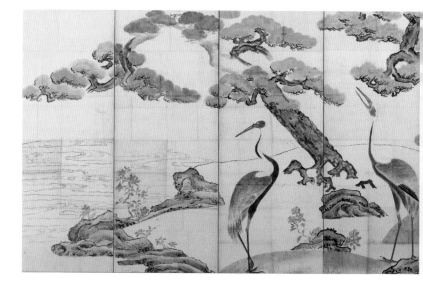

Ogata Kōrin | *Cranes, Pines, and Bamboo* | EARLY 18TH CENTURY

The Transformation
of a Pine Forest

With their annual leaf fall, beeches create an alkaline
humus that stores a lot of water. The air in this little
forest gradually becomes moister, because the leaves
of the growing beeches reduce the speed of the wind
blowing through the trunks of the pines. Calmer air
meant less water evaporated. More water allowed
the beeches to prosper, and one day they grew up
and over the tops of the pines. In the meantime, the
forest floor and the microclimate had both changed
so much that the conditions became more suited to
deciduous trees than to the more frugal conifers. This
transformation is a good example of what trees can
do to change their environment. As foresters like to
say, the forest creates its own ideal habitat.

Emily Carr | *Among the Firs* | c. 1931

Trees and Aging

A break in its bark, then, is at least as uncomfortable for a tree as a wound in our skin is for us. And, therefore, the tree relies on mechanisms similar to the ones we use to stop this from happening. Every year, a tree in its prime adds between 0.5 to 1 inch to its girth. Surely this would make its bark split? It should. To make sure that doesn't happen, the giants constantly renew their skin while shedding enormous quantities of skin cells. In keeping with trees' size in comparison to ours, these flakes are correspondingly larger and measure up to 8 inches across.

But not every tree sheds in the same way. There are species that shed constantly, then there are others that flake with restraint. In young trees of all species, the outer bark is as smooth as a baby's bottom. As trees age, wrinkles gradually appear (beginning from below), and they steadily deepen as the years progress. The deeper the cracks, the more reluctant the tree is to shed its bark, and this behavior increases markedly with age.

Komatsuya Hyakki | *Cherry Tree and Pheasant* | 1765

83

Aycoobo (Wilson Rodríguez) | *Terraza Ancestral* | 2019

Catching Water

Like many deciduous trees, beeches angle their branches up. Or you could say, down. For the crown opens its leaves not only to catch sunlight but also to catch water. Rain falls on hundreds of thousands of leaves, and the moisture drips from them down onto the twigs. From there, it runs along the branches, where the tiny streams of water unite into a river that rushes down the trunk. By the time it reaches the lower part of the trunk, the water is shooting down so fast that when it hits the ground, it foams up.

⟩ **George Inness** | *Pine Grove of the Barberini Villa* | 1876

Creating a Bubbling Spring

The forest floor acts as a huge sponge that diligently collects all the rainfall. The trees make sure that the raindrops don't land heavily on the ground but drip gently from their branches. The loosely packed soil absorbs all the water, so instead of the raindrops joining together to form small streams that rush away in the blink of an eye, they remain trapped in the soil. Once the soil is saturated and the reservoir for the trees is full, excess moisture is released slowly and over the course of many years, deeper and deeper into the layers below the surface. It can take decades before the moisture once again sees the light of day. Fluctuations between periods of drought and heavy rain become a thing of the past, and what remains is a constantly bubbling spring.

⟨ **Camille Corot** | *Diana and Actaeon (Diana Surprised in Her Bath)* | 1836

Safe Haven

The importance of trees for streams continues even after death. When a dead beech falls
across a streambed, it lies there for decades—
acting like a small dam and creating tiny
pockets of calm water where vulnerable
species can hang out.

⟨ **Johann Heinrich Wilhelm Tischbein** | *A Goose and a Gander
with Their Goslings Honking in Alarm as Two Foxes with Their
Cubs Emerge from the Rushes* | MID-18TH-EARLY 19TH CENTURY

Guarded Treasure

Whenever you walk through a tall, dark forest, you are walking down the aisles of a huge grocery store filled with all sorts of delicacies—at least as far as animals, fungi, and bacteria are concerned. A single tree contains millions of calories in the form of sugar, cellulose, lignin, and other carbohydrates. It also contains water and valuable minerals. Did I say a grocery store? A better description would be a heavily guarded warehouse, for there is no question here of just helping yourself. The door is barred, the bark thick, and you must come up with a plan to get to the sweet treasures inside. And you are a woodpecker.

⟨ **Akseli Gallen-Kallela** | *Great Black Woodpecker* | 1893

Alexis Peyrotte | *A Shepherd Boy* | EARLY 1740S

Sharing Sugar

For many animals, sap-sucking pests such as aphids are a blessing. First, they benefit other insects such as ladybugs, whose larvae happily devour one aphid after another. Then there are forest ants, which love the honeydew the aphids excrete so much that they slurp it up right from the aphids' backsides. To speed up the process, the ants stroke the aphids with their antennae, stimulating them to excrete the honeydew. And to prevent other opportunists from entertaining the idea of eating the ants' valuable aphid colonies, the ants protect them. There's a regular little livestock operation going on up there in the forest canopy. And whatever the ants can't use doesn't go to waste. Fungi and bacteria quickly colonize the sticky coating that covers the vegetation around the infested tree, and it soon gets covered with black mold. Honeybees also take advantage of aphid excretions. They suck up the sweet droplets, carry them back to their hives, regurgitate them, and turn them into dark forest honey. Known as honeydew honey, it is particularly prized by consumers, even though it has absolutely nothing to do with flowers.

An organism that is
too greedy and takes too much
without giving anything in
return destroys what it needs
for life and dies out.

Watanabe Seitei | *Egrets in a Tree at Night* | 1887

Sound Effects

Wood fibers conduct sound particularly well, which is why they are used to make musical instruments such as violins and guitars. You can do a simple experiment to test for yourself how well these acoustics work. Put your ear up against the narrow end of a long trunk lying on the forest floor and ask another person at the thicker end to carefully make a small knocking or scratching sound with a pebble. On a still day, you can hear the sound through the trunk incredibly clearly, even if you lift your head. Birds use this property of wood as an alarm system for their nesting cavities. In their case, what they pick up is not benign knocking but scrabbling sounds made by the claws of martens or squirrels. The sounds can be heard high up in the tree, which gives the birds a chance to escape.

Jasper Francis Cropsey | *Blasted Tree* | 1850

The Importance of Decay

A rotting trunk is home to a complex living community. Wood ants move in and chew the moldy wood to make their papery nests. They soak the nest walls with honeydew, the sugary excretions of aphids. Fungi bloom on this substrate, and their fibrous web stabilizes the nest. A multitude of beetles are drawn to the mushy, rotten interior of the cavity. Their larvae can take years to develop, and therefore, they need stable, long-term accommodations. This is why they choose trees, which take decades to die and, therefore, remain intact for a long time. The presence of beetle larvae ensures that the cavity remains attractive to fungi and other insects, which keep a constant supply of excrement and sawdust raining down into the rot.

W. Herbert Dunton | *Fall in the Foothills* | c. 1933-34

Hibernation

It's late summer, and the forest is in a strange mood. The trees have exchanged the lush green in their crowns for a washed-out version verging on yellow. It seems as though they are getting increasingly tired. Exhaustion is setting in, and the trees are waiting for the stressful season to end. They feel just like we do after a busy day at work—ready for a well-earned rest.

Grizzly bears hibernate. But trees? The grizzly bear is a good candidate for comparison. In summer and early fall, it eats to lay down a thick layer of fat it can live off all winter. And this is exactly what trees do as well. Of course, they don't feed on blueberries or salmon. They fuel themselves with energy from the sun, which they use to make sugar and other compounds they can hold in reserve.

I never tire of watching
tree crowns move back and forth.
I can see both the movement of
the whole community and
the movements of individual trees.

⟩ William Henry Holmes | *Blossoms* | 1927

Vincent van Gogh | *Green Wheat Field with Cypresses* | 1889

Gustav Klimt | *Beech Grove I* | 1902

Time, Sight, and Memory

In many latitudes, forests drop leaves in the fall and leaf out in the spring, and we take this cycle for granted. But if we take a closer look, the whole thing is a big mystery, because it means that trees need something very important: a sense of time. How do they know that winter is coming or that rising temperatures aren't just a brief interlude but an announcement that spring has arrived? Beeches don't start growing until it is light for at least thirteen hours a day. That in itself is astounding, because to do this, trees must have some kind of ability to see.

How do trees register that the warmer days are because of spring and not late summer? The appropriate reaction is triggered by a combination of day length and temperature. Rising temperatures mean it's spring. Falling temperatures mean it's fall. Trees are aware of that as well. And that's why species such as oaks or beeches, which are native to the Northern Hemisphere, adapt to reversed cycles in the Southern Hemisphere if they are exported to New Zealand and planted there. And what this proves as well, by the way, is that trees must have a memory. How else could they inwardly compare day lengths or count warm days?

A Question of Character

On a country road stand three oaks growing unusually close together: mere inches separate the one-hundred-year-old trunks. Their interconnecting crowns form a single large dome. The closely spaced trunks could all be growing from the same root, as happens sometimes if downed trees start to regrow. However, the triad of fall color points to a very different story. When the oak on the right is already turning color, the middle one and the one on the left are still completely green. It takes a couple of weeks for the two laggards to follow their colleague into hibernation.

But if their growing conditions are identical, what accounts for the differences in their behavior? The tree on the right is a bit more anxious than the others, or to put it more positively, more sensible. What good are extra provisions if you can't shed your leaves and have to spend the whole winter in mortal danger? So, get rid of the lot in a timely manner and move on to dreamland! The two other oaks are somewhat bolder. Who knows what next spring will bring, or how much energy a sudden insect attack might consume and what reserves will be left over afterward? Therefore, they simply stay green longer and fill the storage tanks under their bark and in their roots to the brim. The timing of leaf drop, it seems, really is a question of character.

⟩ **Claude Monet** | *The Bodmer Oak,*
Fontainebleau Forest | 1865

Natural Pesticides

Trees keep hidden reserves of energy on hand to fight off pests. These secret reserves can be activated at any time, and depending on the tree species, they contain a selection of defensive compounds produced by the tree. These so-called phytoncides have antibiotic properties. A biologist from Leningrad, Boris Tokin, wrote that if you add a pinch of crushed spruce or pine needles to a drop of water that contains protozoa, in less than a second, the protozoa are dead. In the same paper, Tokin reported that the air in young pine forests is almost germfree, thanks to the phytoncides released by the needles. In essence, then, trees disinfect their surroundings.

⟨ **Sandow** | *Pine Tree* | N.D.

1883

116

Lost Seeds

Mice, squirrels, and jays tuck into the oily, starchy seeds on the forest floor as winter provisions. Sometimes a hungry tawny owl or a yellow-necked mouse might end up eating the remains, making its contribution to the next generation of trees, small though it might be.

⟨ **George Elbert Burr** | *Untitled (Trees in Snow)* | 1883

Optimism

I am not anxious when I think about the future of our forests. On large continents, species have to come to grips with new arrivals all the time. Migrating birds bring small animals, fungal spores, or the seeds of new species of trees tucked in their feathers, or these organisms are blown in by turbulent storms. A five-hundred-year-old tree has surely had a few surprises in its life. And thanks to the great genetic diversity in a single species of tree, there is always a sufficient number of individuals that can rise to a new challenge. And thanks to the incredible ability to learn and remember, old trees are like an anchor in the storm of time. They pass on all their experience hereditarily to their offspring.

⟨ **William Morris** | *Cock Pheasant* | 1916

Clean Air

The air truly is considerably cleaner under trees, because their leaves and needles hang in a steady breeze, catching large and small particles as they float by. Not only do trees filter materials out of the air, they also release substances into it. They exchange scent-mails and, of course, pump out germ-killing phytoncides.

Korean scientists have been tracking older women as they walk through forests and urban areas. The result? When the women were walking in the forest, their blood pressure, their lung capacity, and the elasticity of their arteries improved, whereas an excursion into town showed none of these changes. It's possible that phytoncides have a beneficial effect on our immune systems as well as the trees' health, because they kill germs. Personally, however, I think this swirling cocktail of tree talk is the reason we enjoy being out in the forest so much.

⟨ **Henri Rousseau** | *The Banks of the Bièvre near Bicêtre* | c. 1908-9

Street Kids

Urban trees are pampered and primped the first few decades of their lives. Sometimes they even have their own personal irrigation lines and customized watering schedules. In their new territory, they're in for a big surprise. The roots of forest trees don't actually grow very deep. That's not a problem in the forest, where there is almost no limit as to how wide the roots can grow. Unfortunately, this isn't the case on the side of the street. The roadway restricts growth in one direction, there are pipes under the pedestrian zones, and soil has been compacted during construction.

In such places, plane trees, maples, and lindens feel out underground wastewater pipes. We notice the damage when the next storm comes and the streets fill with water. Then specialists armed with root probes investigate to see which tree has caused the blockage. The culprit is sentenced to death for its excursion under the sidewalk and into what it thought was paradise.

The offending tree is cut down, and its successor is planted in a built-in root cage to discourage such behavior in the future.

Why do trees grow into pipes in the first place? For a long time, city engineers thought the roots were somehow attracted by moisture seeping from loose connections between the pipes or by nutrients in the wastewater. However, the results of an extensive applied study by the Ruhr University Bochum point in a completely different direction. The study found the roots in the pipes were growing above the water table and did not seem interested in extra nutrients. What was attracting them was loose soil that had not been fully compacted after construction. Here, the roots found room to breathe and grow. It was only incidentally that they penetrated the seals between individual sections of pipe and eventually ran riot inside them.

Tosa Mitsuoki | *Flowering Cherry and*
Autumn Maples with Poem Slips | 1654-81

Sahibdin | *Krishna and Radha in a Bower:*
Page from a Dispersed Gita Govinda | c. 1665

The Spectrum

Why is the world full of color anyway? Sunlight is white, and when it is reflected, it is still white. And so we should be surrounded by a clinical-looking, optically pure landscape. That this is not what we see is because every material absorbs light differently or converts it into other kinds of radiation. Only the wavelengths that remain are refracted and reach our eyes. Therefore, the color of organisms and objects is dictated by the color of the reflected light. And in the case of leaves on trees, this color is green.

Henri Rousseau | *Portrait of a Woman in a Landscape* | 1890s

Green Shadows

The chlorophyll leaves use for photosynthesis has a so-called green gap, and because leaves can use just a little bit of this part of the color spectrum, they reflect most of it back unused.

Although many shades of color are filtered out in the forest canopy—for example, very little red and blue make their way through—this is not the case for the color green. Because the trees can't use it, some of it reaches the ground. Therefore, the forest is trans-fused with a subdued green light that just happens to have a relaxing effect on the human psyche.

Life in the Slow Lane

The main reason we misunderstand trees is that they are so incredibly slow. Their childhood and youth last ten times as long as ours. Their complete life-span is at least five times as long as ours. Active movements such as unfurling leaves or growing new shoots take weeks or even months. And so it seems to us that trees are static beings, only slightly more active than rocks. It's hardly any wonder that many people today see trees as nothing more than objects.

⟨ **Paula Modersohn-Becker** | *Girl in a Birch Forest* | c. 1903

Frederic Edwin Church | *Forest in Jamaica* | 1865

Breaking Down Barriers
between Animals and Plants

We are part of Nature, and we can survive only with the help of organic substances from other species. We share this necessity with all other animals. The real question is whether we help ourselves only to what we need from the forest ecosystem, and—analogous to our treatment of animals—whether we spare the trees unnecessary suffering when we do this.

That means it is okay to use wood as long as trees are allowed to fulfill their social needs, to grow in a true forest environment on undisturbed ground, and to pass their knowledge on to the next generation. And at least some of them should be allowed to grow old with dignity and finally die a natural death.

In the forest, the
diversity of animal life
plays out mostly in the
microscopic realm,
hidden from the eyes
of visitors.

Abbott Handerson Thayer and **Richard S. Meryman**
Peacock in the Woods, Study for Book
Concealing Coloration in the Animal Kingdom | 1907

Connections

Just how important this interconnected global network of forests is to other areas of Nature is made clear by this story from Japan. Katsuhiko Matsunaga, a marine chemist at Hokkaido University, discovered that leaves falling into streams and rivers leach acids into the ocean that stimulate the growth of plankton, the first and most important building block in the food chain. More fish because of the forest? The researcher encouraged the planting of more trees in coastal areas, which did, in fact, lead to higher yields for fisheries and oyster growers.

⟨ **Ando Hiroshige** | *Temple Gardens in Nippori* | 1857

Appendix: Deeper Wisdom

The abridged quotes within these pages have been extracted from the book *The Hidden Life of Trees* by Peter Wohlleben. For further exploration, we have provided cross-references to the passages from the original English-language version of the book.

Credits

The publisher would like to kindly thank the museums, libraries, archives, galleries, photographers, and artists for their permission to reproduce the works in this book. Every effort has been made to trace all copyright owners. Should any have been inadvertently overlooked, the publisher would be pleased to make the update at the first opportunity. All images accessed online in May of 2023.

Cover Metropolitan Museum of Art, New York. Mr. and Mrs. Isaac D. Fletcher Collection, Bequest of Isaac D. Fletcher, 1917. Acc no.: 17.120.214.

1 Metropolitan Museum of Art, New York. Bequest of Collis P. Huntington, 1900. Acc no.: 25.110.6.

2–3 Metropolitan Museum of Art, New York. Harry G. Sperling Fund, 2006. Acc no.: 2006.339.

4 Metropolitan Museum of Art, New York. Gift of Mrs. John A. Rutherfurd, 1914. Acc no.: 14.141.

6 Metropolitan Museum of Art, New York. Purchase, C.G. Boerner Gift, 2008. Acc no.: 2008.264.

8 Metropolitan Museum of Art, New York. Purchase, Morris K. Jesup Fund, Martha and Barbara Fleischman, and Katherine and Frank Martucci Gifts, 1999. Acc no.: 1999.19.

10 Smithsonian American Art Museum, Washington. Transfer from the U.S. National Museum. Obj no.: 1953.3.4.

13 Courtesy National Gallery of Art, Washington. Gift of Mrs. John Alexander Pope. Rosenwald Collection. Acc no.: 1950.1.85.

14 Smithsonian American Art Museum, Washington. Bequest of Olin Dows. Acc no.: 1983.90.236.

16 Kunstmuseum Basel, Switzerland. Acc no.: Inv. 2225.

18 SMK, National Gallery of Denmark, Copenhagen. 1891–2. Inv no.: KMS8914.

20 Metropolitan Museum of Art, New York. Gift of Paul-Yves Sébillot, 1949. Acc no.: 49.114.

22 Metropolitan Museum of Art, New York. Purchase, Joseph Pulitzer Bequest, 1939. Acc no.: 39.81.1.

24 Metropolitan Museum of Art, New York. Harry G. Sperling Fund, 2006. Acc no.: 2006.329.

26 Courtesy Tropenbos International, Bogotá, Colombia. One from series of twelve. © 2009–10.

28 Musée d'Orsay, Paris. Bought with the help of an anonymous Canadian donation, 1980. Inv no.: RF 1980-195.

30 Metropolitan Museum of Art, New York. Purchase, Gift of Raymonde Paul, in memory of her brother, C. Michael Paul, by exchange, 1985. Acc no.: 1985.237.

32 Smithsonian American Art Museum, Washington. Bequest of Mabel Johnson Langhorne. Acc no.: 1956.11.58.

34 Rijksmuseum, Amsterdam. Gift of G.A. de Graag, 1935. Obj no.: RP-P-1935-926.

36 Courtesy Macaulay & Co. Fine Art, Vancouver, BC. Photograph © Barb Choit. The McMichael Canadian Art Collection.

40-41 Art Institute of Chicago. Joseph Winterbotham Collection. Ref no.: 1923.308.

42 Art Institute of Chicago. Sara R. Shorey Endowment. Ref no.: 1996.3.

44 Courtesy Open Art Images. Collection Golestan Palace, Tehran.

46 Metropolitan Museum of Art, New York. Rogers Fund, 1920, transferred from the Library. Acc no.: 1991.1073.44.

49 Metropolitan Museum of Art, New York. Gift of Irwin Untermyer, 1964. Acc no.: 64.101.1305.

50 Smithsonian American Art Museum, Washington. Museum purchase. Acc no.: 1984.48.

52 Metropolitan Museum of Art, New York. Harry G. Sperling Fund, 2009. Acc no.: 2009.406.

54 Smithsonian American Art Museum, Washington. Bequest of Helen Hayes Smith. Acc no.: 2009.31.1.

56 Metropolitan Museum of Art, New York. Harry G. Sperling Fund, 2006. Acc no.: 2006.340.

59 Metropolitan Museum of Art, New York. The Mr. and Mrs. Henry Ittleson Jr. Purchase Fund, 1956. Acc no.: 56.13.

60 Smithsonian American Art Museum, Washington. Gift of Mahonri Sharp Young. Acc no.: 1978.1101.

62 Metropolitan Museum of Art, New York. The Elisha Whittelsey Collection, the Elisha Whittelsey Fund, 2006. Acc no.: 2006.338.

64-65 Metropolitan Museum of Art, New York. Van Day Truex Fund, 2006. Acc no.: 2006.343.

66 Courtesy National Gallery of Art, Washington. Collection of Mr. and Mrs. Paul Mellon. Acc no.: 1985.64.8.

68 Art Institute of Chicago. Margaret Day Blake Collection. Ref no.: 1976.22.

70 The Cleveland Museum of Art. Leonard C. Hanna, Jr. Fund. Acc no.: 1988.19.

72 Metropolitan Museum of Art, New York. Rogers Fund, 1949. Acc no.: 49.30.

75 Cooper Hewitt, Smithsonian Design Museum, New York. Gift of Mrs. F. Hopkinson Smith. Acc no.: 1923-41-25.

76 Metropolitan Museum of Art, New York. Purchase, Barbara and William Karatz Gift and funds from various donors, 2004. Acc no.: 2004.139.

78 Metropolitan Museum of Art, New York. The Harry G.C. Packard Collection of Asian Art, Gift of Harry G.C. Packard, and Purchase, Fletcher, Rogers, Harris Brisbane Dick, and Louis V. Bell Funds, Joseph Pulitzer Bequest, and The Annenberg Fund Inc. Gift, 1975. Acc no.: 1975.268.62, .63.

80 Glenbow Museum Collection, Calgary. Purchased 1955. Acc no.: 139A.

83 Art Institute of Chicago. Clarence Buckingham Collection. Ref no.: 1925.2147.

84 Courtesy the artist and Instituto de Visión, Bogotá, Colombia.

86-87 Metropolitan Museum of Art, New York. Gift of Lyman G. Bloomingdale, 1898. Acc no.: 98.16.

88 Metropolitan Museum of Art, New York. Robert Lehman Collection, 1975. Acc no.: 1975.1.162.

90 Metropolitan Museum of Art, New York. Purchase, Didier Aaron Inc. Gift, 2003. Acc no.: 2003.111.

92 Ateneum Art Museum, Finnish
    National Gallery, Helsinki. Owner:
    Suomen Valtio. Photograph © Hannu
    Aaltonen. Inv no.: A-1996-2.

94 Cooper Hewitt, Smithsonian Design
    Museum, New York. Gift of Elea-
    nor and Sarah Hewitt. Acc no.:
    1921-22-260.

97 Rijksmuseum, Amsterdam. Gift of
    the Firma Ferwerda en Tieman, 1914.
    Obj no.: RP-P-1914-4656.

98 Metropolitan Museum of Art,
    New York. Charles Stewart Smith
    Collection, Gift of Mrs. Charles
    Stewart Smith, Charles Stewart
    Smith Jr., and Howard Caswell
    Smith, in memory of Charles
    Stewart Smith, 1914. Acc no.:
    14.76.61.42.

100 Art Institute of Chicago. Gift of
    Jamee J. and Marshall Field. Ref no.:
    1997.898.

102 Smithsonian American Art Museum,
    Washington. Transfer from the U.S.
    Department of the Interior, National
    Park Service. Acc no.: 1965.18.36.

105 Smithsonian American Art Museum,
    Washington. Gift of Dr. Anna Bartsch
    Dunne. Acc no.: 1962.4.18.

106 Metropolitan Museum of Art, New
    York. Purchase, The Annenberg
    Foundation Gift, 1993. Acc no.:
    1993.132.

108 Galerie Neue Meister, Dresden.
    Acquired in 1912 from the Great Art
    Exhibition in Dresden via the H.O.
    Miethke Gallery, Vienna, with funds
    from the Proell-Heuer Foundation.
    Inv No.: Gal.-Nr. 2479 A.

112-13 Metropolitan Museum of Art, New
    York. Gift of Sam Salz and Bequest of
    Julia W. Emmons, by exchange, 1964.
    Acc no.: 64.210.

114 Smithsonian American Art
    Museum, Washington. Transfer
    from the U.S. Department of the
    Interior, National Park Service. Obj
    no.: 1969.64.10.

116 Smithsonian American Art
    Museum, Washington. Bequest of
    Carolann Smurthwaite, in memory
    of her mother, Caroline Atherton
    Connell Smurthwaite. Obj no.:
    1983.83.45.

118 Birmingham Museums, Birming-
    ham, UK. Photo by Birmingham
    Museums Trust. Obj no.: 1947M55.

120 Metropolitan Museum of Art, New
    York. Gift of Marshall Field, 1939.
    Acc no.: 39.15.

124-25 Art Institute of Chicago. Kate S.
    Buckingham Endowment. Ref no.:
    1977.156-157.

126 Metropolitan Museum of Art, New
    York. Gift of Ernest Erickson Foun-
    dation, 1988. Acc no.: 1988.103.

128 The Barnes Foundation, Philadel-
    phia. Acc no.: BF260.

130 Museum voor Schone Kunsten
    Gent, Belgium. Bequest of Tony
    Lasnitzki, 1991. Inv no.: 1991-I.

132 Cooper Hewitt, Smithsonian
    Design Museum, New York.
    Gift of Louis P. Church. Acc no.:
    1917-4-679-c.

135 Smithsonian American Art
    Museum, Washington. Gift of the
    heirs of Abbott Handerson Thayer.
    Acc no.: 1950.2.11.

136 Art Institute of Chicago. Gift of Mr.
    and Mrs. Harold G. Henderson. Ref
    no.: 1965.1015.

145 The New York Public Library. The
    Miriam and Ira D. Wallach Division
    of Art, Prints and Photographs:
    Picture Collection. ID no.: 1704192.

⟩ **Arthur Rackham** | *Fairies Are All
More or Less in Hiding until Dusk* | 1913

Greystone Books Ltd. | greystonebooks.com
David Suzuki Institute | davidsuzukiinstitute.org

Cataloguing data available from Library and Archives Canada
ISBN 978-1-77840-140-4 (cloth)
ISBN 978-1-77840-141-1 (epub)

Editing by Michelle Meade
Proofreading by Alison Strobel
Cover and interior design by Jessica Sullivan
Cover image: Narcisse-Virgile Diaz de la Peña,
Autumn: The Woodland Pond, 1867

Printed and bound in China on FSC® certified paper at
Shenzhen Reliance Printing. The FSC® label means that materials
used for the product have been responsibly sourced.

Greystone Books thanks the Canada Council for the Arts,
the British Columbia Arts Council, the Province of British
Columbia through the Book Publishing Tax Credit, and the
Government of Canada for supporting our publishing activities.

Greystone Books gratefully acknowledges the xʷməθkʷəy̓əm (Musqueam),
Sḵwx̱wú7mesh (Squamish), and səlilwətaɬ (Tsleil-Waututh) peoples on
whose land our Vancouver head office is located.

DAVID SUZUKI INSTITUTE